ELECTRIC RAILW

TO THE "DAILY MAIL" WATERPLANE

TO DAY FLIGHTS BY GRAHAME-WH

VOLK'S ELEC
CORBE HRE
RUNNING AN
AT PL
OVER T
FROM PALACE P
RETURN
FARE: 4

BRIGHTON

VOLK'S ELECRING RAILWAY
The "DAILY MAIL"
HYDRO-AEROPLANE
HANGAR
PASTON PLACE STATION
JULY 23-29

VOLK'S
ELECTRIC
RAILWAY

SWEETS.   J. PALMER.   MINERALS.   TEA

TEAS

SUPERIOR
ICE CORNETS 2 1

SUPER
ICE COR

MILK

ROLL & BUTTER 2
LARGE CUP TEA 2
NEW MILK 1
LEMONADE · GINGERBEER 1

CUP TEA 2
NEW MILK 1
LEMONADE 1

COUNTY BOROUGH OF BRIGHTON

A CENTURY *of*
BRIGHTON
& HOVE

Bateman's striking shop front in East Street, Brighton, *c.* 1905. Note the Pickfords removals van with its solid tyres. (*Christopher Samuelson*)

A CENTURY *of* BRIGHTON & HOVE

DAVID ARSCOTT

SUTTON PUBLISHING

First published in the United Kingdom in 2000 by Sutton Publishing Limited

This new paperback edition first published in 2007 by
Sutton Publishing, an imprint of NPI Media Group
Cirencester Road · Chalford · Stroud · Gloucestershire · GL6 8PE

British Library Cataloguing in Publication Data
A catalogue record for this book is available from the British Library.

ISBN 978-7509-4907-1

Front endpaper: Volk's Railway station in the 1920s. (*Brighton Local Studies Library*)

Back endpaper: Brighton station, *c.* 1933, when electrification brought swift and frequent services between London and the coast. (*Brighton Local Studies Library*)

Half-title page: Bathing chalets on the beach in 1929. Undressing in public view was not allowed. (*James Gray Collection*)

Full-title page: Magnus Volk's amazing 'Daddy-Long-Legs', *c.* 1900, shortly before it closed. The car, which had a decorated saloon with a promenade deck above, carried passengers on tracks set into the chalk foreshore from Rottingdean to the terminus of Volk's Electric Railway by the Banjo Groyne. (*Brighton Local Studies Library*)

*For Doreen Darby,
and in fond memory of Ben*

Typeset in Photina.
Typesetting and origination by
Sutton Publishing.
Printed and bound in England.

Contents

West Street, Brighton, at the turn of the century, with the tower of St Paul's church an unmistakable landmark. (*Brighton Local Studies Library*)

Britain: A Century of Change

Two women encumbered with gas masks go about their daily tasks during the early days of the war. (*Hulton Getty Picture Collection*)

The sixty years ending in 1900 were a period of huge trans-
formation for Britain. Railway stations, post-and-telegraph offices,
police and fire stations, gasworks and gasometers, new livestock
markets and covered markets, schools, churches, football grounds,
hospitals and asylums, water pumping stations and sewerage plants
totally altered the urban scene, and the country's population tripled
with more than seven out of ten people being born in or moving to the
towns. The century that followed, leading up to the Millennium's end in
2000, was to be a period of even greater change.

When Queen Victoria died in 1901, she was measured for her
coffin by her grandson Kaiser Wilhelm, the London prostitutes put on
black mourning and the blinds came down in the villas and terraces
spreading out from the old town centres. These centres were reachable
by train and tram, by the new bicycles and still newer motor cars,
were connected by the new telephone, and lit by gas or even electricity.
The shops may have been full of British-made cotton and woollen
clothing but the grocers and butchers were selling cheap Danish bacon,
Argentinian beef, Australasian mutton and tinned or dried fish and fruit
from Canada, California and South Africa. Most of these goods were
carried in British-built-and-crewed ships burning Welsh steam coal.

As the first decade moved on, the Open Spaces Act meant more parks,
bowling greens and cricket pitches. The First World War transformed
the place of women, as they took over many men's jobs. Its other
legacies were the war memorials which joined the statues of Victorian
worthies in main squares round the land. After 1918 death duties and
higher taxation bit hard, and a quarter of England changed hands in
the space of only a few years.

The multiple shop – the chain store – appeared in the high street:
Sainsburys, Maypole, Lipton's, Home & Colonial, the Fifty Shilling Tailor,
Burton, Boots, W.H. Smith. The shopper was spoilt for choice, attracted
by the brash fascias and advertising hoardings for national brands like
Bovril, Pears Soap, and Ovaltine. Many new buildings began to be seen,
such as garages, motor showrooms, picture palaces (cinemas), 'palais
de dance', and ribbons of 'semis' stretched along the roads and new
bypasses and onto the new estates nudging the green belts.

During the 1920s cars became more reliable and sophisticated as well
as commonplace, with developments like the electric self-starter making
them easier for women to drive. Who wanted to turn a crank handle
in the new short skirt? This was, indeed, the electric age as much as
the motor era. Trolley buses, electric trams and trains extended mass
transport and electric light replaced gas in the street and the home,
which itself was groomed by the vacuum cleaner.

A major jolt to the march onward and upward was administered by
the Great Depression of the early 1930s. The older British industries

– textiles, shipbuilding, iron, steel, coal – were already under pressure from foreign competition when this worldwide slump arrived. Luckily there were new diversions to alleviate the misery. The 'talkies' arrived in the cinemas; more and more radios and gramophones were to be found in people's homes; there were new women's magazines, with fashion, cookery tips and problem pages; football pools; the flying feats of women pilots like Amy Johnson; the Loch Ness Monster; cheap chocolate and the drama of Edward VIII's abdication.

Things were looking up again by 1936 and new light industry was booming in the Home Counties as factories struggled to keep up with the demand for radios, radiograms, cars and electronic goods, including the first television sets. The threat from Hitler's Germany meant rearmament, particularly of the airforce, which stimulated aircraft and aero engine firms. If you were lucky and lived in the south, there was good money to be earned. A semi-detached house cost £450, a Morris Cowley £150. People may have smoked like chimneys but life expectancy, since 1918, was up by 15 years while the birth rate had almost halved.

In some ways it is the little memories that seem to linger longest from the Second World War: the kerbs painted white to show up in the

A W.H.Smith shop front in Beaconsfield, 1922.

blackout, the rattle of ack-ack shrapnel on roof tiles, sparrows killed by bomb blast. The biggest damage, apart from London, was in the south-west (Plymouth, Bristol) and the Midlands (Coventry, Birmingham). Postwar reconstruction was rooted in the Beveridge Report which set out the expectations for the Welfare State. This, together with the nationalisation of the Bank of England, coal, gas, electricity and the railways, formed the programme of the Labour government in 1945.

Times were hard in the late 1940s, with rationing even more stringent than during the war. Yet this was, as has been said, 'an innocent and well-behaved era'. The first let-up came in 1951 with the Festival of Britain and there was another fillip in 1953 from the Coronation, which incidentally gave a huge boost to the spread of TV. By 1954 leisure motoring had been resumed but the Comet – Britain's best hope for taking on the American aviation industry – suffered a series of mysterious crashes. The Suez debacle of 1956 was followed by an acceleration in the withdrawal from Empire, which had begun in 1947 with the Independence of India. Consumerism was truly born with the advent of commercial TV and most homes soon boasted washing machines, fridges, electric irons and fires.

Children collecting aluminium to help the war effort, London, 1940s. (*IWM*)

A street party to celebrate the Queen's Coronation, June 1953. (*Hulton Getty Picture Collection*)

The *Lady Chatterley* obscenity trial in 1960 was something of a straw in the wind for what was to follow in that decade. A collective loss of inhibition seemed to sweep the land, as the Beatles and the Rolling Stones transformed popular music, and retailing, cinema and the theatre were revolutionised. Designers, hairdressers, photographers and models moved into places vacated by an Establishment put to flight by the new breed of satirists spawned by *Beyond the Fringe* and *Private Eye*.

In the 1970s Britain seems to have suffered a prolonged hangover after the excesses of the previous decade. Ulster, inflation and union troubles were not made up for by entry into the EEC, North Sea Oil, Women's Lib or, indeed, Punk Rock. Mrs Thatcher

applied the corrective in the 1980s, as the country moved more and more from its old manufacturing base over to providing services, consulting, advertising, and expertise in the 'invisible' market of high finance or in IT.

The post-1945 townscape has seen changes to match those in the worlds of work, entertainment and politics. In 1952 the Clean Air Act served notice on smogs and pea-souper fogs, smuts and blackened buildings, forcing people to stop burning coal and go over to smokeless sources of heat and energy. In the same decade some of the best urban building took place in the 'new towns' like Basildon, Crawley, Stevenage and Harlow. Elsewhere open warfare was declared on slums and what was labelled inadequate, cramped, back-to-back, two-up, two-down, housing. The new 'machine for living in' was a flat in a high-rise block. The architects and planners who promoted these were in league with the traffic engineers, determined to keep the motor car moving whatever the price in multi-storey car parks, meters, traffic wardens and ring roads. The old pollutant, coal smoke, was replaced by petrol and diesel exhaust, and traffic noise.

Punk rockers demonstrate their anarchic style during the 1970s. (*Barnaby's Picture Library*)

Fast food was no longer only a pork pie in a pub or fish-and-chips. There were Indian curry houses, Chinese take-aways and American-style hamburgers, while the drinker could get away from beer in a wine bar. Under the impact of television the big Gaumonts and Odeons closed or were rebuilt as multi-screen cinemas, while the palais de dance gave way to discos and clubs.

From the late 1960s the introduction of listed buildings and conservation areas, together with the growth of preservation societies, put a brake on 'comprehensive redevelopment'. The end of the century and the start of the Third Millennium see new challenges to the health of towns and the wellbeing of the nine out of ten people who now live urban lives. The fight is on to prevent town centres from dying, as patterns of housing and shopping change, and edge-of-town supermarkets exercise the attractions of one-stop shopping. But as banks and department stores close, following the haberdashers, greengrocers, butchers and ironmongers, there are signs of new growth such as farmers' markets, and corner stores acting as pick-up points where customers collect shopping ordered on-line from web sites.

Millennium celebrations over the Thames
at Westminster, New Year's Eve, 1999.
(*Barnaby's Picture Library*)

Futurologists tell us that we are in stage two of the consumer revolu-
tion: a shift from mass consumption to mass customisation driven by
a desire to have things that fit us and our particular lifestyle exactly,
and for better service. This must offer hope for small city-centre shop
premises, as must the continued attraction of physical shopping,
browsing and being part of a crowd: in a word, 'shoppertainment'.
Another hopeful trend for towns is the growth in the number of young
people postponing marriage and looking to live independently, alone,
where there is a buzz, in 'swinging single cities'. Their's is a 'flats-and-
cafés' lifestyle, in contrast to the 'family suburbs', and certainly fits in
with government's aim of building 60 per cent of the huge amount of
new housing needed on 'brown' sites, recycled urban land. There looks
to be plenty of life in the British town yet.

Brighton & Hove: An Introduction

L ike the many actors who have trodden the boards of its famous
Theatre Royal, Brighton has endlessly reinvented itself, rising
above the occasional booing and hissing to earn the ready
applause of an audience which enjoys a bravura performance, a licensed
naughtiness and a touch of pantomime. Hove, its westerly neighbour,
may traditionally have affected a much more sober demeanour, but by
the end of the twentieth century the two towns had fused administrat-
ively and were together engaged in a vigorous campaign for city status.

Superficially the century had begun with a saunter of grace and
elegance – those photographs of parasolled promenadings are irresistible
– but Brighton's colourful past as a watering place for the wealthy
was already proving a mixed blessing. Away from the flamboyant
Georgian and Victorian seaside architecture (the gaudy Royal Pavilion,
the Theatre Royal, the Aquarium, the piers, the Grand and Metropole
Hotels) there were rank dens of overcrowded poverty.

The resort so successfully promoted by Dr Richard Russell in the
1750s for its health-giving sea water (his patients were not only to swim

Fred Collins and one of his
speedy *Skylark* yachts,
c. 1900. A local guide
described the captain as
'most agreeable company',
adding that 'enlivened with
song, jest, anecdote and
instrumental music, his
trips are universally voted
as being very enjoyable'.
(*Brighton Local Studies
Library*)

13

A publicity poster for
Southern Railways, *c.* 1930.
(*Royal Pavilion, Libraries &
Museums, Brighton & Hove*)

in it, but to drink it, too) and so fashionably linked with the excesses of
George, the Prince Regent, was not the 'tiny fishing village' of popular
imagination but a major Sussex town fallen upon hard times. Because
of its cheap land and its willing pool of unemployed labour it was ripe
for redevelopment, and – further boosted by the coming of the railway
to 'London-by-the-Sea' in 1841 – it expanded at a frightening pace. The
population rose from 7,000 at the beginning of the nineteenth century
to 123,000 a hundred years later. By 1921 Brighton was the second
most densely populated county borough in the country.

Medieval Brighton had been largely contained within the area bordered
by North, West and East streets, with the parish church of St Nicholas
(patron saint of fishermen) on its hill to the north-west. Hove had
been concentrated around Hove Street: until Victorian times sheep grazed
on the land where Grand Avenue was to be laid out, and a piggery
adjoined Palmeira Square. Now the two towns spread rapidly towards
each other, with handsome terraces along the front (Kemp Town in
Brighton, Brunswick in Hove), and poorer, denser areas of houses on
former open fields (known as laines) on the outskirts. The laines had
been subdivided into furlongs, and many of the new streets were
superimposed upon their boundaries: major thoroughfares such as
Western Road and St James's Street follow the line of ancient tracks
across agricultural land.

The Victorians had been the first to tackle the problems brought about by overcrowding, building new sewers, introducing a clean water supply and, in about 1876, clearing slums in the Tichborne Street area off Church Street – a quarter then renowned for its drunks, thieves and prostitutes. All too soon, however, it was time to start again. Graham Greene's 1938 novel *Brighton Rock* captured, albeit with some exaggeration, a genuine squalor. The town's seafront gaiety and opulence – attracting an influx of day-trippers by train on a scale scarcely conceivable today – contrasted vividly with the deprivation all too evident in its run-down terraces.

But if the 1920s and '30s in Brighton are in part remembered for the razor-wielding protection gangs at the racecourse, for the gruesome trunk murders which earned the resort the soubriquet 'the Queen of Slaughtering Places' and for the notorious 'dirty weekend' (with would-be divorcees fixed up with a prostitute and a convenient witness), they were also a time of impressive public provision: better housing, improved roads, cheap and reliable transport. The First World War over, Brighton Corporation began the development of what was to become the borough's largest housing estate, at Moulsecoomb (the semi-detached houses with their large gardens in South Moulsecoomb were regarded by some as the 'homes fit for heroes' called for by Lloyd George) with another, similar development in the Queen's Park area. Further estates followed in the 1930s, among them Whitehawk, and government subsidies led to extensive slum clearances in areas such as Carlton Hill, Upper Bedford Street and Upper Russell Street.

At this crucial period the town was blessed with men of vision, the most outstanding of them being Sir Herbert Carden, 'the maker of modern Brighton'. He spent a considerable amount of his own fortune to buy large areas of surrounding downland, enabling the huge extension of the borough boundaries in 1928, when 'Greater Brighton' was created. Under his leadership Brighton Corporation launched such municipal enterprises as the trams and the telephone network.

The next 'great rebuilding' began only after another war had passed, a war fought much closer to home than the first. There were 56 air raids on Brighton between July 1940 and March 1944, claiming 198 lives and seriously injuring 357 people. German pilots driven away from their intended inland targets would often drop their bombs on coastal towns as they turned for home. Since Hitler had chosen Sussex to the east of Brighton as one of the chief invasion areas, it has been suggested that the attacks on the town, which had no obvious military targets, were also in part an advance softening-up exercise. In any event, they served to demolish some 200 houses and damage 15,000 more, about a thousand of them severely.

Many of the sweeping changes to the townscape of the 1960s and '70s now seem to stem not only from a need to replace and improve,

Brighton's Saturday morning market in Upper Gardner Street, 1960. (*Ben Darby*)

but from an architectural over-confidence – a smug view that modern technology's gift of high-stress concrete and plate glass necessarily produced superior buildings. Certainly Brighton and Hove both bear the ugly scars of the period, not only in the form of intrusive, unimaginative tower blocks, but in areas of wasteland – notably by Brighton railway station and off Jubilee Street, near the Corn Exchange – which have remained undeveloped into the early twenty-first century. Among the few successes was the University of Sussex, designed by Sir Basil Spence as one of the new wave of postwar campuses, but the public declined to fall in love with such newcomers as the Brighton Centre and the Kingswest complex on the seafront, while the proudly heralded Churchill Square shopping precinct (for which, amazingly, the Grand Hotel itself was almost sacrificed) soon became regarded as an uncomfortable eyesore and was replaced by a new mall just before the century's end.

Today Brighton displays its usual contradictions. Its detractors point to its perennial areas of poverty, a pervasive run-down appearance (a complaint most often made by locals) and the gaggles of beggars on its streets – many of them finding understandable refuge from less attractive surroundings in other parts of the country. Those who love it relish its continuing raffishness, the vitality of its pubs and clubs, its air of tolerance, the freedom it seems to allow its inhabitants to become, within limits, whatever they wish to be: it is no coincidence that Brighton should be the unofficial gay capital of England.

Visually there is variety, too. Close to the handsome Regency façades of Lewes Crescent and Sussex Square at the eastern end of the seafront lies Brighton Marina, an ambitious artificial yacht harbour first built in the 1970s, but extended subsequently on a site which covers all of 127 acres. The approach is through a barbaric concrete road interchange, and the distance of the 1500 moored boats from the shops, houses, restaurants and cinema complex is perhaps a missed opportunity, but the development can be read as a dramatic, and popular, statement of the town's restless modernity.

It is also, of course, a reminder of the importance of the sea. Other parts of the town certainly attract visitors in droves (the narrow Lanes with their antiques and jewellery shops, the Royal Pavilion with its wonderful over-the-top oriental fantasies), but it is the seafront which epitomises the Brighton experience. Contrast again: the twentieth century ended with the beautiful West Pier in a state of seemingly terminal decay, awaiting the millions of pounds that would be needed to save it, but the lower promenade had been rejuvenated with new shops, cafés, a night club and a small fishing museum occupying its seafront arches, while the Palace Pier, also freshly revamped, laid claim to being one of the most visited tourist attractions in the country.

How, finally, to characterise Brighton? A bit of a chancer, perhaps, not too comfortable to live with, but full of energy and with a wicked sense of humour. Definitely not the sort to introduce to your prim and proper maiden aunt without due warning, but immensely popular with the younger, and wilder, members of the family. Rather loud, up all hours of the night and warmly generous without caring too much whether you return the affection – but you almost certainly will.

John Bright's shop at 24 Western Road, 1901. This was a competition window, as the poster at the top reveals, but magnificent displays such as this were common in upmarket shopping areas. (*Hove Library*)

Edwardian Brighton
& Hove

The West Pier, *c*. 1900. Brighton began the century with two piers and the wreck of a third – the old Chain Pier, a glorified landing stage for passengers to and from Dieppe, which had been destroyed by a storm in December 1896. The magnificent West Pier, designed by the famous pier architect and engineer Eugenius Birch, was opened in October 1866, some thirty-three years before the Palace Pier half a mile to the east. The Hotel Metropole, commanding the seafront in this photograph, is Brighton's largest and dates from 1890. (*Brighton Local Studies Library*)

King's Road, Brighton, opposite the Grand Hotel, 1900. The carriage road and promenade had been laid out in 1822 to replace a rough track inaccessible to traffic, and in this picture it still has something of a rustic feel. The Italian-style Grand, built in the 1860s, was the most elegant of the town's hotels, with Hobden's Royal Baths ('swimming taught' reads the sign) directly connected to it. The baths, first established in 1813 to treat gout with a vacuum pump, were demolished in 1908 to make way for the hotel ballroom. (*Brighton Local Studies Library*)

Locomotive sheds, Brighton station *c.* 1900. The London, Brighton & South Coast Railway was the town's major employer at the beginning of the century, with a locomotive manufacturing works, a foundry, maintenance and repair shops, carriage-painting shops and a marine engineering works for the company's cross-Channel fleet, which together required a workforce of around 2,600. A gradual decline culminated in the demolition of the buildings in 1969, the site ending the century as a much argued-about car park which had been long awaiting its developer. (*Robert Jeeves*)

Rediscovering the Goldstone, 1900. 'The Tolmen or Holy Stone of Druids. Col-chor or Godstone of Ancient Britons' reads an inscription close to the present site of this 20-ton monster. Whatever it was once used for, the impressive rock (a greywether of the kind to be seen at Stonehenge) so fascinated archaeologists and the general public when it lay on farmland at Goldstone Bottom during the nineteenth century that they regularly opened the farmer's gates and trampled his crops to gaze at it. Unamused, he had a huge hole dug to bury it, and it lay hidden for more than half a century until William Hollamby, a Hove commissioner, hit upon the idea of resurrecting it – eventually having it shifted to Hove Park for its opening in May 1906. Here we see the team of labourers who carried out the task of disinterment on 29 September 1900. (*Hove Library*)

Devil's Dyke Cable Railway, *c.* 1900. You have to peer hard, but there are passengers in that cage being carried 230 feet above the valley bottom. The Dyke has always been a popular recreational spot for Brightonians, and at the beginning of the century the place was abuzz with movement: the Dyke Railway ran here from Brighton; there was a steep-grade railway down the steep scarp face of the Downs to Poynings; and there was also a short 'roller-coaster' close to the Devil's Dyke Hotel. The cable railway closed in about 1909, but the concrete footings of its two pylons can still be seen. (*Hove Library*)

Fitting tram rails in Lewes Road, Brighton, 1901. Trams were introduced to the town in November of this year, the initial terminus being at the southern end of Victoria Gardens. Passengers were charged a penny for any distance they took along the route via Lewes Road to Preston Barracks. By 1904 there was a 9½ mile system in operation, but the greater flexibility of buses was to bring about its demise in 1939. (*James Gray Collection*)

Preston Circus, 1901. The Hare & Hounds pub still stands, but at the time this snow scene was photographed the imposing building at the centre was about to be demolished to make way for the laying of tram lines beween Beaconsfield Road and Viaduct Road. Formerly Longhurst's Brewery, it ended its life as a 'manufactory' of mineral waters. (*Christopher Samuelson*)

The Palace Pier, *c.* 1901. Opened to the public in May 1899, the Palace Pier was at first nothing but a simple decking with an illuminated entrance archway and a series of pretty filigree arches. Within two years, however, it had its oriental pier pavilion, including a concert hall, and it added new attractions throughout the century – becoming one of the most visited tourist venues in the country. (*Christopher Samuelson*)

North Street, *c.* 1902. Looking down the street from the clock tower at a time when walking in the road was no hazard. Horse-buses were first introduced in 1840, and this double decker, pulled by two horses, could carry twenty-six passengers in addition to its rather bored looking conductor. Note how plastered it is with advertisements on every available surface. (*Christopher Samuelson*)

William IV public house, Bond Street entrance, 1904. One would love to know what event these men, with their array of flat caps, boaters, bowlers and buttonholes, were off to. This was the heyday of pubs in Brighton. A little earlier, in 1889, there were 774 of them – one for every 130 residents. (*Christopher Samuelson*)

Brighton's first bus, 1904. These were heady times for Arthur Dunn, who worked for Brighton, Hove & Preston United Omnibus Company as a horse-bus driver, but who on 1 January 1904 drove the first bus to Brighton from the Milnes Daimler Works in Tottenham Court Road, London. For the first few weeks of the year he was the only motor-bus driver in town. (*Brighton Local Studies Library*)

Old Ship Hotel in Motor Week, 1905. Brighton had a special place in early motoring. The first veteran car run from Brighton had been staged in 1896 to celebrate the Act of Parliament which allowed speeds of up to 12mph and scrapped the requirement for vehicles to be preceded by a man with a red flag, and in July 1905 the first National Speed Trials took place on the new tarmac surface of Madeira Drive. The Old Ship Hotel, the town's oldest inn, was the favourite venue of 'sporting motorists', and the home of the Automobile Club. The Peugeot at the centre-right of the picture has an early number plate, A75, the A signifying London. The Daimler on the right is a relative upstart, with an A8065 plate. (*Christopher Samuelson*)

Election posters, 23 Bath Street, Brighton, 1905. This busy wall captures a significant moment in both local and national politics. Gerald Loder, one of the town's two members of Parliament since 1889, had just been appointed Lord of Treasury, and that meant he had to submit himself to the voters once more in a by-election. This took place on Wednesday 5 April 1905 and, sensationally, he was defeated by his Liberal opponent, Ernest Villiers. It was a sign of things to come: by December the Tories had surrendered office to the Liberals without first going to the polls, and in the General Election which followed early in 1906 the Liberals had a landslide victory. (The former Tory leader Arthur Balfour lost his seat, while in Brighton Villiers was returned alongside fellow Liberal Edward Risdale.) The posters carry messages uncomfortably characteristic of a party in disarray, with calls for military might and a hostility towards immigrants. (*Brighton Local Studies Library*)

Royal Mail transport, 1905. These two scenes, both posed outside the Ship Street head post office in the same year, need no words to emphasise their significance. The motor mail coach was the very first from London to Brighton, on 1 June 1905. Although it spoke of progress (do we only imagine that the younger members of the team seem to regard themselves as proud harbingers of a new age?), it's interesting to observe the continuity in design, with a railed, tarpaulined section on top. (*Brighton Local Studies Library*)

C.A. Sharp, butchers, promotional postcard, *c.* 1905. This shop, on the south side of Western Road towards the border with Hove, was clearly no place for vegetarians. Southdown mutton was still a speciality, with vast flocks covering the treeless Downs between Eastbourne and Steyning. Today the Southdown is a rare breed. (*Christopher Samuelson*)

Edwardian promenade, Hove, *c.* 1906. It may look like a film set for *My Fair Lady*, but this was a common sight on the Brunswick Lawns, particularly after church on Sunday mornings. The sun shone, a military band played and the local press prepared fashion notes with which to enchant its female readers: 'Of striking appearance was Mrs Tyndall Robertson's costume of black charmeuse, with hat of rose du Barri feathers.' They must have thought it was never going to end. (*Hove Library*)

Fire at St Peter's Church, Preston, 1906. Preston was once a small and separate village a little more than a mile north of Brighton, and its listed church, adjacent to Preston Manor, dates from around 1250. In the nave there are the remains of medieval wall paintings, but these were damaged, with much else, by the fire which gutted the church on 23 June 1906. (*Brighton Local Studies Library*)

Spring Street, Brighton, *c.* 1906. Dating old photographs is often difficult, but this one offers a few useful clues. The placard on the pavement features 'curious accident of Brighton Motor Mail' which (*see p. 27*) places it between June 1905 and the demise of the Larkin's leather goods shop on the right of the picture not very long afterwards. Spring Street, which runs north off Western Road, still contains many of its artisan cottages from the 1820s. The sign for Hampton Street, on the left beyond the Shakespeare's Head, is missing its 'H'. (*Christopher Samuelson*)

George Street, Hove, 1907. The view north from Church Road towards Blatchington Road long before the controversial pedestrianisation introduced at the end of the century would have crossed anyone's mind. Shaw's Store on the right later became the Army & Navy. The fishmonger's shop next door belonged to Edward Hayden. (*Hove Library*)

Pictorial Centre, Queen's Road, Brighton, *c.* 1907. Rudolph Handwerck was the proprietor of this famous shop at a time when postcards were being produced in a quantity and variety never known before or since. (*Christopher Samuelson*)

Hove seafront, *c.* 1907. 'A bird's eye view of Hove' is how the postcard publisher described what today seems a strange sight. This was the view from Courtenay Terrace, with private gardens running down to the beach. (*Hove Library*)

Travellers Joy Inn, Hove, 1908. Time was running out for the Travellers Joy in Alma Terrace when this photograph was taken. One of the earliest pubs in Hove, it was demolished during this year to make way for the St Aubyn's Hotel. The horse in the doorway and the two dogs are obviously exceedingly obedient: the child with the teddy bear, mercifully, finds it impossible to keep still. (*Hove Library*)

King's Road, Brighton, 1909. A major improvement to the seafront road is under way and is due to take some little time: a spanking new tarmacadam surface will be inaugurated on 22 July the following year. (*Brighton Local Studies Library*)

Edward VII memorial procession, 1910. Massive crowds turned out for the King's memorial service on 20 May, the day he was buried at St George's Chapel, Windsor. Here the Corporation and public bodies of Hove process up the Drive on their way to the parish church. Every head is covered. (*Hove Library*)

High Street, Portslade, *c.* 1910. Portslade was amalgamated with Hove in 1974, but that would have seemed improbable in the early years of the century when the village still had memories of being larger than its neighbour. Its self-sufficiency is suggested by the large 'provision store' sandwiched between two pubs, the Stag's Head and the George Inn. The village had its own brewery, too. The so-called Swiss Cottages at the back of the picture, one of them with a smoking chimney, were part of the Portslade Farm estate and managed to survive into the 1960s. Portslade village was declared a conservation area in 1974. (*Hove Library*)

Royal Pavilion, *c.* 1910. The Prince Regent's oriental palace is perhaps the most photographed building in Brighton and Hove, but this is an unusual view, with a bandstand erected on the lawn fronting the Old Steine and a festooning of large paper lanterns. (*Christopher Samuelson*)

Peacock Lane, Brighton, *c.* 1910. There is still a country lane feeling to Peacock Lane, off the London Road in the Withdean area, but in this delightful view the road remains unmetalled and it is evidently safe to stroll near the middle of it. (*Christopher Samuelson*)

Crowds leaving the Goldstone Ground, Good Friday, 1910. Not a hooligan in sight, but this was, after all, one of Brighton & Hove Albion's glory seasons – indeed, perhaps the most successful ever. Formed as Brighton and Hove Rangers in 1900, the club changed its name when it turned professional a year later. The Rangers home ground had been at Surrenden Field, Withdean, but the Albion played first at the County Ground in Hove in the 1901/2 season and then moved to the Goldstone Ground the following season. In the 1909/10 season the Albion won the Southern League championship, the Southern Charity Cup and – at Stamford Bridge – the FA Charity Shield, their 1–0 victory in the latter over Football League champions Aston Villa earning them the unofficial title 'Champions of All England'. A replica of the Charity Shield is set into the gable of 238 Dyke Road, built for a director of the Albion, Noah Clark. (*Hove Library*)

The Pepperpot, *c.* 1912. Thomas Attree bought Queen's Park in about 1825, the year after it was first laid out as a subscription pleasure garden. Apart from commissioning the architect of the Houses of Parliament, Sir Charles Barry, to design him a grand villa close by (it was demolished in 1972), he had an Italianate temple (now listed) built in his garden and the so-called Pepperpot or Pepperbox, complete with Corinthian pillars and cupola, erected where Queen's Park Road meets Junction Road. Its original purpose is, strangely, unknown. It may have been an observation tower (it was used as such in the Second World War), a water tower or, more humbly, a sewer vent, but it is certainly, in its elevation of design above mere function, a cousin to the county's numerous follies. Ten sided, and standing 60 ft high, it has subsequently had various uses, at one time being the print works for the *Brighton Daily Mail*. (*Christopher Samuelson*)

Brighton Race Course, *c.* 1912. The fact that only one of these photographs shows the sails still attached to the dilapidated post mill on the race course reveals that they were taken at different times, but both certainly date from before 1913, by which time it had been dismantled. (It had first stood on Albion Hill in about 1822, but was moved to the Race Hill in December 1861.) The earliest race meetings in the area had been at Lewes, a few miles away, but in 1783 the Duke of Cumberland, the Marquess of Queensberry and other prominent inhabitants of the town organised the first races on this breezy hilltop site, and the patronage of the Prince of Wales ensured their early fashionability. Brighton Races had their low point in the 1920s and 30s, when they became notorious for the viciousness of London protection gangs, but ended the century in fine fettle, with the company which leases the course from the local authority spending freely to improve the facilities. (*James Gray Collection*)

Western Road, 1912. A scene looking east along the town's principal shopping street. The domed building which dominates it (nos 49–55) was built for Knight & Wakeford, the drapers, in 1903. Although it looks wide enough at this spot, the road had developed rapidly from being a narrow track between North Street and Hove Church, and the steady encroachment of buildings prompted the corporation to begin buying properties in 1906 for a road widening which was eventually carried out during the 1920s and '30s. (*Christopher Samuelson*)

Hove's new motor fire engine, 1914. A great day for the borough, with the usual display of hierarchy: the brave firemen in their burnished helmets play second fiddle to the civic dignitaries who swarm all over their new toy. (*Hove Library*)

Trolley bus, 1914. This was an experiment that failed. The solid-tyred Cedes-Stoll gearless trolley bus, powered by overhead electric wires, ran from Hove station to Goldstone Villas, George Street and Church Road, where it is seen here. Never used by the public, it was clean and quiet (apart from the loud hissing it made when it stopped), but it failed to impress local councillors and was withdrawn. (*Hove Library*)

James Edward's 'Hove Outfitting Mart', 1915. It seems generous of Edwards to yield an important part of his frontage to an advertisement for another store, and perhaps he thought so, too: a photograph taken a few years later shows that he had replaced it with one of his own. The premises were on the corner of Church Road and George Street, one of Hove's main shopping areas. (*Hove Library*)

The
First World War

Brighton volunteers, 1914. A young girl shields her eyes from the sun's glare to watch a posse of men en route for the recruitment office. Britain had declared war on Germany on 4 August. (*Brighton Local Studies Library*)

Wounded soldiers at Brighton Grammar School, 1914. The horror of war was brought home to the public very quickly, with the return home of the first casualties – men of the 2nd Royal Sussex Regiment wounded during the retreat from Mons. Three hundred men were taken to the new Brighton, Hove and Sussex Grammar School (now the Sixth Form College), requisitioned by the military as the 2nd Eastern General Hospital. Men, women and children flocked to watch them. (*Brighton Local Studies Library*)

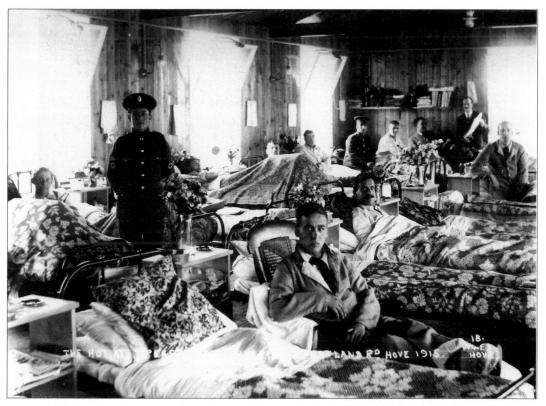

'The Hut', Hove, 1915. As the number of the injured continued to rise, emergency beds had to be found. This was the 2nd Eastern General Hospital's annexe in Portland Road. (*Hove Library*)

Wounded Indian soldiers in the Pavilion grounds, 1915. Within three months of the outbreak of war the number of Indian casualties at the Front already numbered some 1,800. Brighton was chosen as one of the towns to care for the wounded, with hospitals at the Royal Pavilion, Dome and Corn Exchange; at the Brighton Workhouse (later Brighton General Hospital) in Elm Grove; and at the York Place schools. For those well enough to appreciate the irony, the reminders of home in the shape of Prinnie's oriental minarets was perhaps mildly amusing. (*Brighton Local Studies Library*)

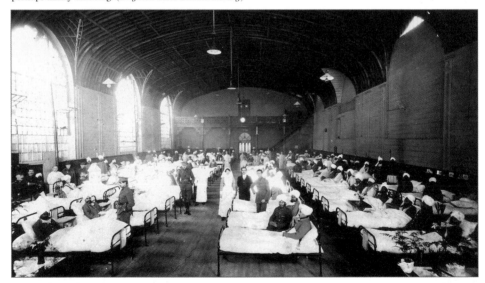

Corn Exchange as an Indian hospital, 1915. As an open space, the Corn Exchange was easily converted into a hospital, but Major Lelean from the War Office discovered that the Pavilion was a crowded museum and that the Dome had 1,500 seats clamped to its tiers. Fortunately forty members of the Boys' Brigade ('sturdy young fellows', reported the *Gazette*) set about clearing away the exhibits and removing the seats in a single Saturday night. (*Brighton Local Studies Library*)

Wartime refuse collection, *c.* 1917. During the war it was all hands to the pump – or, at least, to the Harrop-Roller seen here in Ditchling Road, Brighton. The driver was William Thomas, but the names of the five conscripted women and the old-time 'regular' are lost to us. War didn't always bring out the best in people. When the workhouse was cleared of its inmates to make way for wounded soldiers, many people attempted to resist the influx of sick and old to their neighbourhoods. (*Brighton Local Studies Library*)

Children's peace celebrations, 1919. They think it's all over – and so it is, for another twenty years. This event is probably taking place in Hove Park. During the war Hove collected £289,620 in National War Bonds and Savings Certificates, and in acknowledgement the town was in 1919 awarded its own tank, 'Hova', which sat in the park until 1937. (*Hove Library*)

45

The Chattri, 1921. On 1 February the Prince of Wales attended the unveiling and dedication of the Indian memorial high on the Downs above Patcham. Constructed of white Sicilian marble, it was raised within a 2-acre garden at the spot where the bodies of soldiers who died in the town had been cremated during and immediately after the First World War. The inscription reads: 'To the memory of all the Indian soldiers who gave their lives in the service of their King-Emperor this monument, erected on the site where the Hindus and Sikhs who died in hospital at Brighton passed through the fire, is in grateful admiration and brotherly affection dedicated.' The South Gate of the Royal Pavilion is another memorial of the same period, dedicated for the use of the inhabitants of Brighton by His Highness the Maharajah of Patiala on 26 October 1921. (*Brighton Local Studies Library*)

Between the Wars

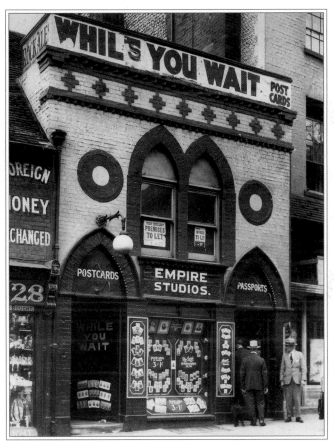

29 North Street, *c.* 1930. 'Step inside and be photographed now' encourages a sign in the window of Empire Studios. There seems to be a queue, perhaps for 'postcards of yourself' at three for a shilling. The building on the right, faced with cream-coloured mathematical tiles, is Clarence House, named for William IV, formerly the Duke of Clarence, and at this period a hotel. (*Christopher Samuelson*)

Boot and shoe repairers, *c.* 1920. Most of the tightly packed terraces in the Hanover area of Brighton date from the 1860s. This is no. 10, with a typical angular window bay. The owners clearly needed to use every last inch of space to make ends meet because, apart from using part of the ground floor as a boot repair business, they have put a 'Room to let' notice in the window. (*Christopher Samuelson*)

Dyke Road, *c.* 1920. It's rather difficult to believe that Dyke Road was as rural as this at so late a date, but building development alongside the northern stretch of the road was only just under way at this period. This spot is close to Tivoli Crescent North. Until the early nineteenth century when the Cuckfield–London Road route was inaugurated, this had been the main route into Brighton from the north. (*Christopher Samuelson*)

Upper Russell Street, Brighton, *c.* 1920. This is a view which has completely disappeared. The Artillery Arms on the near right of the photograph stood on the corner of Artillery Street. The area already has something of a run-down appearance in the photograph, and by 1938 the first clearance of dilapidated buildings began with a view to creating a new shopping heart for the town. In the 1960s this long-delayed scheme became the Churchill Square development – and the area in the picture is now part of the car parks under the shopping mall. (*Christopher Samuelson*)

Family butcher, 57a Richmond Street, *c.* 1920. The Albion Hill area, north of Grand Parade, was one of Brighton's poorest in the early years of the century, and this display outside the Hills butcher's shop (with what appears to be a snoozing pig) is noticeably humbler than others to be found in these pages. Richmond Street was once the steepest road in the borough, with railings across its width part-way down to stop runaway carts, and it climbed vertiginously to Windmill Street. The street sign on the wall at the left reveals that our butcher had his premises at the junction of Richmond Street and Windmill Terrace, and above the door the faded words WINDMILL HOUSE can just be deciphered, so this was close to the highest point: the delivery boys must have hoped not to bring anything back with them after their errands downhill. There had been windmills in the area in the past, but none survived at this time. The area was partly cleared of its slums in the 1930s, and in the 1960s Brighton's first tower-block homes were built here. (*Christopher Samuelson*)

Moving George IV, 1922. The statue of 'Prinnie' is a familiar sight today outside the northern gate of his Royal Pavilion, but it originally stood in the northern enclosure of the Old Steine. Here a tractor of the Southern Transport Company hauls it away to make room for the town's new war memorial. (*James Gray Collection*)

Unveiling the war memorial, 1922. On 7 October Admiral of the Fleet Earl Beatty unveiled the memorial to the 2,600 Brightonians who perished during the First World War. It was designed, fittingly, by a Brighton-born architect: John W. Simpson, president of the RIBA from 1919 to 1921. After the official wreaths had been laid huge numbers of people came forward with their own floral tributes, completely covering the memorial. At such a time of heightened emotion, it is hardly surprising to learn that thirty people fainted. (*James Gray Collection*)

August Bank Holiday in the rain, 1922. Proof that sun didn't always shine in days gone by, although that was evidently no deterrent to visitors: the line of motor-coaches stretches away into the distance. The widening of Madeira Drive in 1929 would move the terminus of Volk's Electric Railway a little away from its original site, seen here, while the Aquarium ('Thousands of live specimens', reads a sign beneath its clock) would be rebuilt at the same time. (*James Gray Collection*)

The Palladium Cinema, 1922. This fine-looking building
has been replaced by the Kingswest complex on the
seafront. Built in 1888 as the Alhambra Opera House and
Music Hall, it reopened in 1912 with seating for 1,200
as the Grand Cinema de Luxe or Palladium Cinema. It
was splendid inside, too, with balustrades and cupolas, an
ironwork canopy and a roof which could be opened in fine
weather. (*Brighton Local Studies Library*)

Philbrock's, 11 Victoria Terrace, Hove, 1922. Why the best wishes were being extended to customers at this
time isn't recorded, but this was a succulent display by what was one of the town's most venerable butcher's
shops, founded in the 1850s. (*Hove Library*)

Prestonville Garage, *c.* 1922. The telephone number is a Hove one, but this garage was, as its name implies, in Prestonville Road, off the Seven Dials in Brighton. The car with the Hackney Carriage disc over its number plate is a Daimler. The face at the window suggests that posing by the vehicles was regarded as man's work. (*Christopher Samuelson*)

Fire escape demonstration, *c.* 1922. In December 1920 a bad fire at the corner of Duke Street and West Street in Brighton led to biting criticism of the police and volunteer brigades. The upshot was the disbanding of this service and the creation of a full-time and well-trained corporation fire brigade, housed at Preston Circus from May 1921. Here we witness what seems to be a public relations exercise, convincing the public that the town's new Morris-Magirus turntable fire escape is a fitting answer to the critics. (*Christopher Samuelson*)

Unic taxi, Surrey Street, Brighton, *c.* 1922. None too smart, perhaps (only two of his four buttons are done up), but this driver must have been a jolly companion. He is posing outside the *Evening Star*, a pub conveniently close to Brighton station and still in existence today. (*Christopher Samuelson*)

Electric Empire Cinema, Hove, *c.* 1923. Those pioneers of film George Albert Smith and James Williamson made their first films in Hove at the end of the nineteenth century, but the town erected a barrier to the enjoyment of picture-goers: unlike its neighbours in Brighton, Portslade and Southwick, it refused cinemas permission to open on Sundays. Here we see a crowd of excited youngsters outside the cinema at 76–7 George Street. Child star Jackie Coogan is the attraction, in *Long Live the King*. (*Hove Library*)

Duke of York's Cinema, Preston Circus, *c.* 1923. Unlike the Electric Empire, the Duke of York's was purpose built as a luxury cinema in 1910 (on the site of the brewery building pictured on page 23), and it is today the oldest in Brighton. The silent pictures were accompanied variously by an orchestral piano, an American organ and a powerful gramophone. (*Christopher Samuelson*)

Terminus Hotel, 1924. The Queen's Road approach to Brighton station had become too congested by the 1920s, and this picture was taken in the year that the Terminus Hotel and the Flowing Stream in Surrey Street were demolished to allow the construction of Junction Road. Ten years later this narrow link road would itself have to be widened. (*Christopher Samuelson*)

Dyke Railway, *c.* 1924. The lines have gone today, but it is still possible to make out the platform which marks the end of the line for the conventional railway climbing from Brighton to Devil's Dyke between 1887 and 1938. There were various halts along the way, including one at the golf course: an automatic bell sounded in the clubhouse to warn members that a train was on its way. (*Brighton Local Studies Library*)

Madeira Drive, *c*. 1925. Brilliant holiday weather, with all the hoods of the motor-coaches folded away. Originally known as Madeira Road, the promenade and carriage drive was first constructed in the 1870s, extending from the Palace Pier and Aquarium to a ramp running up to Marine Parade. (*Christopher Samuelson*)

Boating Pool, 1925. Brighton's Lower Esplanade has always been the fish'n'chips, kiss-me-quick stretch of the town, and the putting green and boating pool close to the West Pier (whose decking can be seen behind it) were the new attractions of 1925. (*Christopher Samuelson*)

General Strike, 1926. This is far from being the clearest image in the book, but it freezes a moment in the town's history. The men in uniform outside Brighton Town Hall are special mounted police, known as the Black and Tans, brought in to quell rioting during the General Strike. Public transport had been brought to a standstill, but on 11 May a group of middle-class volunteers, including students, attempted to take trams out of the Lewes Road depot. A large crowd of strikers and their families blocked the entrance, and the Black and Tans attacked them wielding ash staves. The affray became known as the Battle of Lewes Road – a reference to the medieval Battle of Lewes a few miles away. Twenty-two of the workers were imprisoned for their part in the confrontation, whereas the special constables were treated to a civil banquet, the menu including 'Ice bricks à la Lewes Road'. (*James Gray Collection*)

Greater Brighton celebrations, 1928. On 1 April this year Brighton expanded five-fold, to take in Ovingdean, Rottingdean, most of Falmer and parts of Patcham and West Blatchington. There were week-long celebrations. In the leading car in this procession past the Clock Tower are the Duke and Duchess of York, later George VI and Queen Elizabeth. Their visit culminated in the unveiling of the Pylons erected by the A23 to mark the town's northern boundary. (*James Gray Collection*)

Brills Baths, East Street, 1929. Charles Brill had the famous architect Sir George Gilbert Scott design these striking circular baths, then the largest in Europe, in 1869. They held some 80,000 gallons of sea-water, brought in from Hove because Brighton's was thought to be polluted. It was a gentlemen's establishment (Brill had already opened a ladies-only bath) offering a barber and reading- and billiard-rooms as well as a variety of bathing treatments, but by 1929 the taste for such things had passed. Our photograph shows hoardings around it as demolition gets under way – hoardings which, inevitably, are smothered with advertisements. It was replaced by the Savoy Cinema-Theatre. (*James Gray Collection*)

Reconstruction of the Aquarium, 1929. At its inauguration in 1872 the Aquarium was one of the wonders of the age, with the largest display tank in the world and a vaulted interior supported by decorated columns of granite and marble. Apart from the marine wonders within, there was a roof terrace with roller-skating rink, garden, smoking room, café and music conservatory. By the 1920s, however, it had fallen upon hard times and narrowly avoided being turned into a bus and coach station. Here the familiar clock tower is being demolished as part of a major reconstruction, which saw the exterior rebuilt in white Empire stonework and the entrance replaced by two square kiosks with pagoda-style roofs. (*Brighton Local Studies Library*)

King's Road/Grand Junction Road, *c.* 1930. The young lady having trouble with her stockings draws the eye in this picture, but the buildings are of some interest too. The Art Deco one second from the left, with glazed cream terracotta tiles and decorated with Corinthian pilasters, is the Savoy Cinema-Theatre, built on the site of Brill's Baths by Associated British Cinemas. It later became the ABC and the Cannon, but it failed to survive beyond the end of the century. The Palace Pier Hotel hotel next door, formerly Waite's Hotel, housed Tussaud's Waxworks. It was later rebuilt as part of the Royal Albion Hotel. (*Christopher Samuelson*)

Publicity poster, *c.* 1930. Brighton has the ability to be all things to all men – and to this artist it appears to have been a displaced fragment of the Riviera. In the Depression years resorts such as Brighton had to pull out all the stops to attract visitors. (*Royal Pavilion, Libraries & Museums, Brighton & Hove*)

Needhams, Castle Square, 1930. A sad moment for a major clothing store. Robert Needham founded the business in 1848, and the Brighton alderman James Colbourne was its proprietor at the beginning of the century, but here we see it in its last days. It became Electric House. (*Brighton Local Studies Library*)

Beaconsfield Road, Brighton, *c.* 1930. Trams are about to pass in the hazy distance, but otherwise a pram is the only moving thing in sight. The advertisements reveal the lasting nature of several products: Guinness, Chivers' marmalade, Camp coffee, Oxo, Ewbank carpet sweepers. The *Daily Telegraph* cost a penny. (*Christopher Samuelson*)

West Street, Brighton, 1930. The drastic widening of this busy thoroughfare from the Clock Tower to the seafront began in 1928 and had already extended about a third of the way down by the time that this photograph was taken. The corporation removed all of the buildings on the western side apart from St Paul's Church, which was already well back from the road. (*Christopher Samuelson*)

67

King's Road, 1930. The rather improbable huntsmen and their hounds, carefully watched by two police officers, are perhaps on their way to the Preston Park Horse and Dog Show, which is advertised on the van in the centre of the photograph. Tillings were one of the two major bus operators in the town (the other being Southdown), and during this year they introduced a fleet of covered double-decker buses. Among the advertisements on the earlier, open-top model seen here is one for Brighton and Hove Ice Rink, which had opened the previous December in Denmark Villas, Hove. (*James Gray Collection*)

Lewes Road, *c.* 1930. Another almost deserted stretch of road, this at the spot where traffic today masses around the Vogue Giratory system. Bear Road runs off to the left. The railway viaduct in the distance carried trains along the Kemp Town Railway, opened in 1869 and leaving the Lewes line about a mile from Brighton at Kemp Town Junction. It was initially successful, but at the time that this picture was taken it was suffering from competition from the buses, and passenger services were withdrawn in December 1932. Goods traffic continued until 1971, and the viaduct was demolished five years later. (*Christopher Samuelson*)

Motor trials, 1932. Ever since the very first Motor Week in 1905, Madeira Drive has been a stage for fast cars and sporting finishes: the 'Old Crocks' run, the commercial vehicles run, and the London-to-Brighton bicycle ride are just three regular events which today attract crowds which match those seen filling Madeira Terrace in this photograph. (*James Gray Collection*)

Marine Parade, *c.* 1933. This view is taken from the bottom of Marine Parade, close to the Aquarium, before it rises to the east past the splendid Regency architecture of Royal Crescent, Marine Square and Eastern Terrace to the Kemp Town glories of Lewes Crescent and Sussex Square. In the absence of anything quite so grand here, our eye is taken by the splendid Model A Ford on the right. (*Christopher Samuelson*)

Hove Lagoon, *c.* 1933. There was some argument when the Lagoon was created in 1931 between those who found the former tidal mud flats a dreary prospect and those who lamented the destruction of a wildlife habitat. It quickly became a playground for all ages, and was a venue for model yachting events. (*Hove Library*)

Slum clearance in Brighton, 1933. Government funding in the 1930s allowed the corporation to carry out widespread demolition of substandard houses and to build new estates for those who had lived in them. The Carlton Hill area was one of the poorest, and the street below seems all the more wretched for its contrast with the imposing mock-Tudor house in the street opposite. Sun Street, right, was typical in having an open watercourse down the middle of it. (*Brighton Local Studies Library*)

SS Brighton, West Street, 1934. Built on land recently cleared for road widening, and newly opened when this photograph was taken, the SS Brighton began life as a swimming pool but quickly converted to an ice rink when it became clear that people would rather swim in the sea. In its new guise it was immensely popular, and its resident Brighton Tigers ice-hockey team drew large crowds after the war, when it won the British League and other trophies. By this time the building had been relaunched as the Brighton Palladium, with variety shows, concerts and sporting events, but Top Rank bought it in 1962 and within three years closed it down. It was later demolished. (*James Gray Collection*)

Meeting House Lane, Brighton, 1934. A twitten, or alleyway, in the Old Town, close to the Lanes, Meeting House Lane is a cluster of nineteenth-century shopfronts. These are nos 16–18 on the east side. A sketch of the street in 1857 suggests that the shop attracting browsers here was a bookshop even then. (*James Gray Collection*)

Children's film show at The Level, Brighton, 1935. Up goes the back of the van, and an expectant throng waits for the fun to begin. The Level is a traditional venue for fairs and circuses, as well as for public demonstrations. (*Brighton Local Studies Library*)

Embassy Court, King's Road, Brighton, 1935. 'Flats to let' reads the sign on the front of the building, revealing that it has just been completed. This was the first modern high-rise block in the town, and the fact that it stood alongside the Regency elegance of Brunswick Terrace (over the invisible border in Hove) made it controversial, although it is now listed as being of special architectural interest. Note the donkeys: there is very little sand for them on the Brighton and Hove beaches. (*James Gray Collection*)

Jubilee decorations in East Street, Brighton, 1935. The silver jubilee of George V was lavishly celebrated on 6 May 1935, and this is the show put on in East Street. The Royal Pavilion can be glimpsed through all the bunting. (*Brighton Local Studies Library*)

Jubilee decorations, Western Road, 1935. Not to be outdone, Western Road was equally festooned with floral crowns, flags and the royal initials. The view is to the west, Boots the Chemist occupying the neo-classical building on the left by the junction with Dean Street. Until the war it had a restaurant and a resident orchestra. (*Christopher Samuelson*)

No. 12 Grantham Road, 1936. A wonderfully busy shopfront which repays close inspection with a magnifying glass: the *Daily Express* highlights an event it is presumably sponsoring at Ford Aerodrome, the *Daily Mail* is concerned about Prince Henry's marriage tangle, while the Odeon is showing *City of Beautiful Nonsense*, starring Emlyn Williams. Oh, and don't miss the cat! (*Christopher Samuelson*)

District Nurses on their bicycles, Hove, 1937/8. Those Queen's Nurses in their dowdy uniforms in the top picture may have an unworldly air, but they certainly knew how to run a public relations exercise. The local newspaper reported that they had to go off on their rounds from their Wellington Street headquarters on old bicycles: 'An appeal has been issued to provide new machines.' The second picture, a little later, completes the story: 'Presentation of Raleigh bikes to District Nursing Association,' runs the newspaper headline. The mayor, Albert Walter Hillman, did the honours, but one wonders whether Raleigh provided the bikes for the publicity. If so, the company had probably demanded that the nurses dress a little more cheerfully for the picture – and doubtless they were happy to oblige. (*Hove Library*)

Floral Hall, 1938. Another sad loss. The borough engineer Francis May designed this market building between Market Street and Black Lion Street in 1900. The photograph was taken in the year it closed (a new fruit, flower and vegetable market had been opened in Circus Street) and two years before it was demolished and turned into a car park. It had a red-brick and terracotta design, with arched glass and iron roofs. The southern part was the Floral Hall proper, selling flowers, while two other sections dealt in fruit and vegetables. (*James Gray Collection*)

The Second World War

London children were evacuated to Brighton and Hove at the beginning of the war, but once France had fallen to the Germans they were removed to safer parts of the country. (*Brighton Local Studies Library*)

Supreme War Council at Hove, 1939. During the first month of the war the English and French members of the Supreme War Council met in the committee room of Hove Town Hall, which was already heavily sandbagged. The Prime Minister, Neville Chamberlain, stands alone in the centre of the picture, half-turned towards us. The man on the left smoking a cigarette is Admiral Darlan, who later threw in his lot with the pro-German Vichy government, switched sides after the Allied landings in North Africa and was assassinated by a fellow Frenchman on 24 December 1942. (*Hove Library*)

A German pilot's view of Brighton, 1940. This photograph was taken from a German plane flying in over the town, probably on 15 November 1940. The two piers have had lengths of their planking removed to prevent their being used as landing stages in an invasion. (*James Gray Collection*)

Bomb damage, Whitehawk Road, 1940. The first bombing incident in Brighton was on Monday 15 July 1940. A Dornier Do17 flew over at 6 in the morning and dropped bombs on houses in Whitehawk Road, Princes Terrace and Bristol Gardens. Four people were killed and another five seriously injured. (*David Rowland*)

Albion Hill, 1940. No sirens had sounded, and children were playing in the streets, when at about 3.30 in the afternoon of 24 September a Junkers Ju88 dropped its bombs on the tightly-packed terraces in the Albion Hill area. More than thirty houses and the Sir John Falstaff pub were demolished but, amazingly, only two people were killed. (*David Rowland*)

Hanningtons Store, 1940. Mopping up operations on the morning of Saturday 30 November. The previous, foggy evening several enemy aircraft had dropped incendiary bombs and high explosive bombs on the town centre. One of the former crashed into the auditorium of the Savoy Cinema during a performance: 'All but a few patrons, close to where the bomb fell, retained their seats,' the manager told the press, 'and the showing of the film was not interrupted.' Nobody in the town was killed. (*David Rowland*)

Seafront, Hove, *c.* 1940. A grim and moody view of a beach area prepared for invasion. The huge concrete blocks were designed to prevent tank access – but, in the event, all the danger was to come from the air. (*Hove Library*)

Seafront, Hove, *c*. 1940. Another bleak view, with the Hove lawns already become wild and tussocky. A notice on the railings warns that the area is mined. Hitler planned to invade Britain on 24 September of this year, with the Royal Pavilion becoming his southern HQ, but the victory of 'The Few' in the Battle of Britain forced him to change his mind. (*Hove Library*)

Buckingham Close, 1942. At lunchtime on 12 October four Focke-Wulf Fw190s flew over Brighton at about 150 feet, each dropping a 500kg bomb on the town centre. The flats of Buckingham Close were hit by the first of them and three people were killed there. Nine in all died in the raid. (*David Rowland*)

Elder Place, 1942. The third of four bombs dropped on Brighton town centre on 12 October demolished a surface shelter and four houses in Elder Place. An elderly lady was rescued from no. 16, but she was badly injured and died in Brighton General Hospital eleven days later. (*David Rowland*)

Brighton Clinic, Sussex Street, 1943. Just after eleven on the morning of 29 March four Focke-Wulf Fw190s swooped in from the sea at low level, raking the town centre with cannon and machine gun fire and dropping bombs. One of these hit the municipal market in Circus Street, broke through the north wall and exploded in the school clinic in Sussex Street (now Morley Street). Three children and the chief clerk were killed. (*David Rowland*)

Nizells Avenue, Hove, 1943. Ellen Thompson, whose husband Sydney had been mayor of Brighton in 1930, was killed when a bomb demolished her home on 29 March. Dorothy Akehurst, who did housework for Mrs Thompson, died with her. (*Hove Library*)

Bennett Road, Brighton, 1944. After a lull in bombing raids, the so-called 'baby Blitz' began – a concentrated bombing attack on resorts appearing in a wartime guide to places British people liked to visit. This is the scene after bombs fell on East Brighton on the night of 23 February. Eleven people were killed in all, nine of them residents of Bennett Road. (*David Rowland*)

St Nicholas' churchyard, Brighton, 1944. This is the wreckage of a Messerschmitt Me410 which, attacked out at sea by a Mosquito of 92 Squadron, crash-landed in the northern part of the churchyard in the early hours of Tuesday 19 April, carrying bombs which failed to explode. The pilot, 24-year-old Richard Pahl, was killed and is buried in the Bear Road cemetery. The Mosquito pilot, Edward Crew, was one of the best night-fighter aces, surviving the war and leaving the RAF with the rank of Air Vice Marshal. (*Brighton Local Studies Library*)

West Pier, 1945. 'Look, we have come through,' is the unspoken message of this striking photograph. Weary, bowed, but unbroken, these people know that the sea and the skies above it will no longer carry a threat to their very existence. The pier still has a section missing, but it will be open again before the year is out. (*James Gray Collection*)

VE Day in the Lanes, May 1945. Joy unconfined outside English's Oyster Bar as Victory in Europe is celebrated. Fingers under chins urge the photographer to capture the moment for posterity. Why won't that flag unfurl? (*Brighton Local Studies Library*)

Victory Thanksgiving Parade at Hove, 1945. Contingents from HMS *King Alfred* pass the saluting base at the Peace Memorial, leading the parade into Brighton. The lawns are again safe to walk on. (*Hove Library*)

Street party, Grove Street, Brighton 1945. Almost every street in the two towns had a party in May 1945. Money was scarce and food was rationed, but you could still put on a bit of a show, hoist some simple bunting and tog the children out in fancy dress. Prizes for the best, perhaps – but they're all winners here. (*David Rowland*)

The Postwar Period

Sainsbury's store, London Road, *c.* 1955. Meat rationing had ended as recently as 3 July 1954, so that the slogan 'meat every day' had a smack of triumph about it. (*Christopher Samuelson*)

Clock Tower, 1946. 'Any colour as long as it's black' seems to be the dress code – and there wasn't, of course, much choice. The advertisement for savings stamps, with its call to save for the future, distils the sombre post-war mood. The White Lion plaque above the bank remembers the inn which stood on the spot before being demolished for road widening in 1874. (*Christopher Samuelson*)

Period piece, 1949. 'Taken 5 July 1949 at Brighton' says a neat hand on the back of this photograph. 'Babe, Hilda & Mum.' At a time of austerity it was still possible to dress nicely and have a good day out at the seaside. (*Christopher Samuelson*)

Regent Cinema, Queen's Road, 1954. Built in 1921 near the corner with North Street, the Regent was the first of the country's 'super-cinemas', seating some 3,000 people in unaccustomed luxury. Within a couple of years it also had what quickly became a celebrated dance-hall on its roof, and thus became a focal point of Brighton's night life. Its eventual decline followed a familiar pattern: the ballroom became a bingo hall, the cinema closed and, in 1974, the building was demolished. A large and uncompromisingly modern Boots store stands on the spot today. (*Christopher Samuelson*)

The Lanes, 1955. The old buildings which line the twisting twittens of the Lanes were as recently as the 1930s regarded as so run-down that they ought to be demolished, but today, much spruced up, their mixture of specialist shops attracts practically every visitor to the town. (*Ben Darby*)

Rose Garden Pavilion, Preston Park, 1955. The first of Brighton's public parks was purchased in 1883 with cash left to the corporation by the bookmaker William Davies. It covers 63 acres – plenty of room for sporting activities in some areas and, in others, quieter retreats such as this. (*Ben Darby*)

Guinness clock, King's Road, 1956. A nostalgic sight for old Brightonians, but the Swan and the buildings behind it (the Palladium is showing *Who Done It*) are long gone. The Brighton Centre, the town's principal conference and entertainments centre, opened here in 1977. (*Christopher Samuelson*)

Fishermen's Hard, 1956. If these fishermen look somewhat glum it's hardly surprising: they are about to lose a pitch which they and their forebears have enjoyed since at least Tudor times. The council had decided that their market – on the beach between the piers – should be closed on hygiene grounds at the end of the year, moving to a new extension at the Circus Street market. There was a short reprieve, but the fishermen left the site for good in 1960. (*Ben Darby*)

Victoria Fountain, Old Steine, 1956. Amon Henry Wilds, one of the great architects of Regency Brighton and Hove, designed this fountain, which was inaugurated on 25 May 1846 to commemorate the Queen's 27th birthday. It stands at the centre of the Old Steine's southern enclosure. (*Ben Darby*)

Sailing at Brighton, 1957. A view towards the West Pier. The tide is sufficiently low to reveal some sand among the shingle. (*Ben Darby*)

Brunswick Square, Hove, 1958. Brunswick Town, developed in the 1820s and '30s, was then so much closer to Brighton than old Hove that it was commonly referred to as West Brighton. Perhaps Brightonians were simply envious of the beautiful squares and terraces laid out by builder Amon Wilds and architect Charles Busby. After the Second World War the estate was sufficiently run-down for Hove Council to consider demolishing it – an attempted act of vandalism mercifully thwarted by the Regency Society, which was created for just that purpose. (*Hove Library*)

Greenhouses, Stanmer Nurseries, 1959. Brighton's municipal nurseries were one of its less trumpeted glories, although the labours of its gardeners became evident whenever it was time to bed-out in the town's gardens or to bedeck some civic function with flowers. The nurseries, opened in 1957 and incorporating a horticultural training centre from 1966, provided some 70,000 trees and 250,000 hardy plants every year. Alas, they came to be regarded as a luxury, and they closed before the century was out. (*Ben Darby*)

Into the 1960s and '70s

Churchill Square, 1969. Concrete, plate glass and a (very modest) mini-skirt. The new shopping precinct was officially opened in October 1968, at the cost of £9 million and a large number of demolished buildings. (*Doreen Darby*)

Ship Street, 1960. The buildings are unchanged in this elegant old street, but the Silver Grill had become the Reform by the century's end and the Bodega was the Smugglers. (*Christopher Samuelson*)

Banjo Groyne, 1961. The eastward drifting shingle builds up against the promenade groynes, protecting the cliffs against erosion and reclaiming land from the sea. The Banjo Groyne, named for its shape, was built at the eastern end of the front in 1877. By 1884 it had already reclaimed the several acres of land on which the Madeira Lawns were laid out. (*Ben Darby*)

The last Brighton trolley bus run, 1961. They had their devotees, but trolley buses were cumbersome and tended to hold up other traffic. The first, experimental service had been run in April 1939. The same vehicle had the sad honour of taking the very last journey, at 11.30pm on Friday 30 June 1961. (*James Gray Collection*)

Indian summer near the Palace Pier, 1961. Here we see Brighton at its most traditional on a fine September day, with deckchairs claiming the beach and a pleasure boat fast filling up with passengers. Has that dark-suited group in the middle distance taken a wrong turning? (*Ben Darby*)

Building the University of Sussex, 1961. Sir Basil Spence said he was inspired by ancient Greek architecture in designing the colonnades and cloisters of the new university. By November 1961 Falmer House was already taking the shape familiar today. (*Doreen Darby*)

Lower Esplanade, Brighton, 1961. At the very end of the century Brighton at last got to grips with the area below King's Road, improving the arches, laying a handsome new pavement and introducing (sometimes controversial) modern sculpture. Those who refuse to recognise improvement should compare today's seafront with the drabness seen here. (*Ben Darby*)

Pool Valley, 1962. There was, indeed, a regular pool here once, because this is where the Wellsbourne Stream discharged into the sea before it was piped underground. This low-lying area off East Street was first used as a coach station in 1929. Bus services were rather more frequent then. (*Doreen Darby*)

Royal visit to George Street, 1962. The Queen and the Duke of Edinburgh were in Hove on 16 June 1962 to inaugurate improvements to George Street. Here a proud little girl holds out the cushion from which the Queen has just taken scissors to cut the tape. (*Hove Library*)

101

Sea defence works, 1962. The first undercliff walk east from Brighton was created in the early 1930s when the borough engineer designed a sea wall at the base of the cliffs to prevent erosion of the chalk. By 1935 the walk extended to Saltdean Gap, but a further stretch was opened in 1963, and here we see the work under way. The current length of the undercliff walk is now all of 3.35 miles. (*Ben Darby*)

College House, University of Sussex, 1962. The focal point for the university's social activities, this was the first of the buildings to be finished. The initial intake of students arrived in October of this year. (*Doreen Darby*)

Brighton's Saturday morning market, 1963. The authorities first designated Upper Gardner Street as a site for Saturday street trading at the beginning of the century, but it took the tireless work of Harry Cowley to win fixed pitches for the barrow boys. Cowley, who died in 1971, also led a squatting movement after both world wars to give shelter to the homeless. (*Ben Darby*)

No. 1 Edward Street, 1963. The 1960s was a period of rebuilding, and it's surprising to find old stables surviving in such a central part of Brighton as this. By 1990 the site was an office block. (*Doreen Darby*)

Lewes Road, 1963. Not an American streetscape, but the brand new dual carriageway out towards Lewes. The building in the distance was new, too: the ten-storey Cockroft Building of the Brighton College of Technology, now part of Brighton University. (*Doreen Darby*)

Bedford Hotel, King's Road, 1963. Nobody knew it then, but this fine hotel's days were numbered when the photograph was taken. Opened in 1829, it had once been the town's leading hotel, but a fire which damaged the upper storeys in 1964 was a seemingly irresistible excuse to pull it down. Its replacement is modern brutal. (*Doreen Darby*)

Black Lion Street, Brighton, 1963. This is good drinking territory, with the Cricketers Arms, the oldest pub in the town centre, next door to the Black Lion – a reconstruction of the brewery supposed to have been established by the Protestant martyr Deryk Carver. A fat Regency buck is said to have won a bet by boasting that he could beat a younger, fitter man in a race provided that he could choose the course and be given a yard start: he astutely selected Black Lion Lane (the narrow twitten between these two buildings) and therefore couldn't be passed. (*Ben Darby*)

105

Demolition for the creation of Churchill Square, 1963. Plans for a new shopping heart for Brighton were first put forward at the time of the great slum clearances in the 1930s, but it took the iconoclasm of the 1960s to get the job done. A large swathe of land between Western Road and the seafront was rapidly cleared. The picture above looks up West Street from King's Road, with the remains of the Palladium on the left: this corner site would be covered by the Kingswest complex and the Brighton Centre. The picture below looks west from the junction of West Street and King's Road, with the Grand Hotel in the centre. It is scarcely imaginable today, but Brighton Council had intended to pull down the Grand as part of the new development, replacing it with an amusement centre. Our photograph was taken soon after the Government had reprieved it by making it a listed building. (*Ben Darby*)

The Gillette Cup, 1963. Sussex went through the entire century without winning the county championship, but they were the early one-day specialists. The charismatic 'Lord' Ted Dexter, last of the great gentlemen players in the days before the game turned completely professional, lifted the Gillette Cup at Lords in the first season of the competition. Sussex beat Worcestershire in the final. (*Sussex County Cricket Club*)

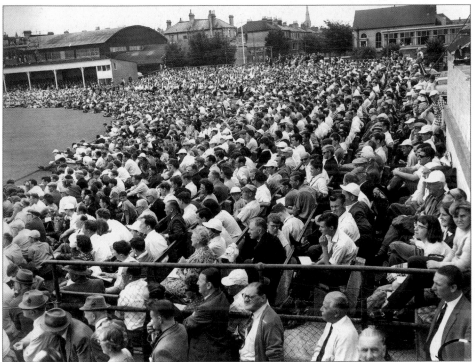

Record crowd at Hove, 1964. Inspired by their 1963 success, the fans turned up to the County Ground in amazing numbers for the following season's competition. This is the scene on 29 July 1964, when a crowd in excess of 15,000 saw Sussex beat Surrey in the semi-final. They went on to take the knock-out cup for the second year in succession, this time overcoming Warwickshire in the final. (*Sussex County Cricket Club*)

Mods and Rockers, 1964. On May Bank Holiday Monday Mods and Rockers achieved legendary status by staging a furious, if relatively harmless, battle on the Aquarium Terrace. The Mods, who wore smart clothes and rode around on motor scooters, are seen attacking the supposedly tougher, leather-clad biker Rockers. A deckchair flies, seemingly unaided, through the air. (*Brighton Evening Argus*)

Pipe-laying in the Victoria Gardens, 1964. The last time trenches had been dug in Brighton's public gardens it had been for war defences, but this time it was to provide water for the lawns and flowerbeds in the summer months. (*Doreen Darby*)

Steine House, 1964. Another close-run thing: at the time of this photograph the former home of Maria Fitzherbert, unofficial wife of the Prince Regent, was scheduled for demolition to make way for a basement shop and storage, parking for sixteen cars, a showroom or banking hall and six floors of offices, but this project was eventually prevented. The YMCA moved into the building in 1884 and has made considerable alterations to it over the years. (*Doreen Darby*)

New dual carriageway, 1965. Road widening has reached the new University of Sussex and the people of Falmer, over the hill, are dreading what will happen next – the bisection of their village by a four-lane highway. Traffic was, of course, considerably lighter a generation ago, but that cyclist does seem to be taking something of a risk. (*Ben Darby*)

109

Hove Town Hall fire, 1966. The architectural writer Sir Nikolaus Pevsner described this building as 'so red, so Gothic, so hard, so imperishable', and within weeks of the words leaving his pen it proved his final adjective horribly wrong. In the early hours of 9 January 1966 it caught fire. Seventy firemen fought the blaze, rescuing six people trapped inside but failing to prevent extensive damage. Not everyone had loved the old place, but it was unquestionably a Victorian masterpiece, designed by Alfred Waterhouse in red brick with terracotta dressings. Its clock tower housed a carillon of twelve bells, which could play fourteen tunes, including Home Sweet Home and God Bless the Prince of Wales. Its Great Hall staged exhibitions and concerts. The replacement town hall failed to please most local residents. (*Hove Library*)

No. 9 Castle Square, Brighton, 1970. An interesting split-personality display, one window spare and understated, the other packed with jars of old-fashioned sweets sold by the quarter. (*Christopher Samuelson*)

Greyhound racing, Hove, *c.* 1974. The Brighton and Hove Stadium opened in June 1928, two years after the sport first took off in Britain. Glen Miner broke the world speed record here on 4 May 1982, covering 563 yards at an average speed of 38.89 mph, while Ballyregan Bob set a new world record of thirty-two successive victories on the evening of 9 December 1986. (*Coral Brighton & Hove Stadium*)

British Engineerium, Hove, 1974. The Goldstone pumping station in Nevill Road was built in 1866 to supply water to the fast-growing metropolis of Brighton and Hove. When it reached the end of its useful life in 1972, Brighton Corporation decided to demolish it. Happily it was listed, and the energetic Jonathan Minns gathered fellow enthusiasts about him to restore the beam engines and other equipment, and to transform the place into a working museum of engineering ingenuity. The British Engineerium was opened to the public on Good Friday 1976. Here we see Minns consulting plans in surroundings which would surely reduce all but the most determined to despair. (*Hove Library*)

Modern Brighton & Hove

Brighton's nudist beach, 1991. Only in England, and perhaps only in Brighton, would there be a demand for naked bathing on forlorn and chilly shingle. The council opened the naturist beach at the eastern end of the seafront below Duke's Mound on 1 April 1980. (*Brighton Evening Argus*)

Athina B, 1980. The fact that all the crew were taken off safely allowed the public to enjoy the spectacle of this shipwreck on the shingle just east of the Palace Pier. The *Athina B*, carrying a cargo of pumice from the Azores, ran aground on 21 January and remained here for almost a month before being towed away to be broken up. Her anchor is on display on the Madeira Drive promenade, above what is now known as the Athina bathing beach. (*James Parr*)

Feeding pigeons by the Peace Memorial, 1986. The man throwing bread stands in Hove and the so-called 'birdcage bandstand' beyond is in Brighton, with the angel of peace marking the boundary between the two. An inscription reads: 'In the year 1912 the inhabitants of Brighton and Hove provided a home for the Queen's Nurses, and erected this monument in memory of Edward VII and as a testimony of their enduring loyalty.' The nurses' home at 12–14 Wellington Road was opened on the same day as the Duke of Norfolk unveiled the memorial. (*Hove Library*)

Grand Hotel, 12 October 1984. At 2.54 in the morning a huge IRA bomb exploded in room 629 of the Grand, the targets being Prime Minister Margaret Thatcher and members of her cabinet who were staying there during the Conservative Party Conference. Five people were killed (none of them MPs) and another thirty-four were injured. Patrick Magee was later convicted of murder, but peace initiatives in Ireland controversially allowed his release from prison with little of his life sentence served. Despite the serious structural damage caused to the building, there was never any doubt that it would be renovated. In the event De Vere Hotels, the owners, decided that the whole building should be revamped in its original style, with a new conservatory added along the length of the ground floor and the creation of Hobdens Health Hydro, commemorating the baths which formerly stood here. Margaret Thatcher herself re-opened the reborn hotel on 28 August 1986, and two years later it became the first five-star hotel in Brighton. (*Christopher Samuelson*)

The Great Gale, 1987. Nobody who lived through it will ever forget the so-called 'hurricane' of October 1987, when a night and early morning of howling winds left five people dead in Sussex (it seemed a miraculously small total) and toppled an estimated five million trees throughout the county. Our top photograph shows the devastation at the Level, with most trees down and the rest little but ruined stumps. The other was taken by the Pavilion Theatre in New Road. The notice innocently warns of a slippery path, a reference to the notoriously perilous droppings from huge flocks of starlings roosting in the trees of the Pavilion grounds. There is little roosting space this morning – and no chance of making that telephone call. (*Brighton Evening Argus*)

Gay Pride, 1998. The leap from prudent concealment to ebullient pride seems to have been remarkably swift, but Brighton's gay community has long been large, effervescent and artistically significant. The annual week-long celebrations culminate in a procession along the seafront and up London Road to Preston Park. (*Brighton Evening Argus*)

Royal Albion fire, 1998. A hapless trainee chef cooking sausages for breakfast set this historic hotel on fire when flames shot up an extraction flue to the roof. The guests were immediately evacuated, but one couple failed to hear the alarm and managed to sleep right through the fire-fighting and beyond. The hotel's prominent position at the corner of the Old Steine and Grand Junction Road did little for the town's image while it awaited repairs, but the owners quickly opted for a complete refurbishment. (*Brighton Evening Argus*)

Cleaning the sewers, 1998. The commodious Victorian brick-lined sewers are among the wonders of Brighton, and they are very much on the tourist map. This balletic scene shows three workers making sure that everything is as clean and decent as possible before the annual influx of subterranean visitors during the Brighton Festival in May. (*Southern Water Services*)

The last goal at the Goldstone, 1999. The disgraceful story of Brighton and Hove Albion's removal from the Goldstone Ground has yet to be told in full. The stadium was sold to a property company which, in turn, sold it on at a much higher price only a short while later, while the club was forced to search desperately for a venue which would satisfy the Football League. The Albion settled for Gillingham in Kent as their home ground for two seasons, before 'coming home' to Withdean Stadium as a further temporary measure while a permanent site could be found. The last match at the Goldstone was an emotional affair for the fans, who saw Stuart Storer score this very last goal in the match against Doncaster on 12 May 1999. (*Brighton Evening Argus*)

French Convalescent Home, 1999. One of the top stories in the last weeks of the century was the threat to the future of this fine building, sitting on land attractive to developers at the Black Rock end of Marine Parade. Linked with the French Hospital in Shaftesbury Avenue, London, it was built for the French Government in 1896 as a convalescent home for poor and aged French nationals living in Britain. After a vigorous campaign by the local newspaper, it was given a reprieve. (*Brighton Evening Argus*)

West Blatchington Windmill, 1999. The new sweeps are swung into position on 26 October 1999, to complete its restoration. A striking (and listed) six-sided smock mill to the north of Hove, it was sketched by Constable in 1825. (*Peter Hill*)

119

Millennium celebrations, Old Steine, 1999/2000. The Victoria Fountain forms part of the backdrop as crowds turn out in huge numbers to celebrate New Year's Eve and the dawn of a new millennium. (*Brighton Evening Argus*)

Acknowledgements

I am immensely grateful to the individuals and organisations who helped me amass the pictures in this book. Notable among the former were Christopher Samuelson, who gave me unrestricted use of his considerable collection, and Doreen Darby, who displayed a similar generosity with the splendid photographs taken by herself and her late husband Ben. Among the latter, I could not have coped without access to the collections held by the Brighton Local Studies Library and Hove Library, where I received sympathetic and expert guidance from Stephanie Green and Zoë Lubowiecka respectively. The *Evening Argus* were an invaluable source of more recent photographs, while, for pictures spanning the larger part of the century, I was privileged to make the first use for a book of this kind of the comprehensive James Gray Collection, owned by the Regency Society of Brighton & Hove and held by the Royal Pavilion, Libraries and Museums, Brighton & Hove: especial thanks here to John Small of the Regency Society and Mark Neathey at the Pavilion. Others who helped with photographs and/or advice included J. Edward Hart, Peter Hill, Jim Parr, Dave Robinson, David Rowland (author of *The Brighton Blitz*) and Robert Jeeves of Branch Two, the Postcard Saloon, while photographers Rob Sanderson and Michael Sullivan provided invaluable copying expertise.

Although I consulted a wide range of books in compiling the captions, *The Encyclopaedia of Brighton* by Timothy Carder must be highlighted as indispensable for anyone researching the history of the town.

SOUTHERN · RAILWAY

LONDON IN ONE HOUR.
TRAINS HOURLY TO LONDON. HAYWARDS HEATH. WORTHING. ETC.
SOUTHERN ELECTRIC

CHEAP FARES
TO LONDON
6/6
EVERY WEEKDAY.

AQUARIUM

13

NJ 5872